The Lighthouse

Glasgow 1999
UK City of
Architecture
and Design

Published on behalf of Glasgow 1999: UK City of Architecture and Design, by:

August
116–120 Golden Lane
London EC1Y OTL
+44 171 689 4400
mail@augustmedia.co.uk

© 1999 August Media Ltd

ISBN: 1 902 854 03 9

Photography:
David Churchill; pages 6, 13, 36–7, 38 (small photo), 43, 44 (small photo), 46–7, 52–3, 58 (small photo), 62, 63
Alan Dimmick; page 16
Andrew Massey; pages 15 (colour photo), 22, 25, 28–9
Anne Odling-Smee; page 26
Phil Sayer, pages 2–3, 8, 11, 38 (large photo), 39, 40–2, 44 (large photo), 45, 48-49, 50–1, 54–7, 58 (large photo), 59–63

Cover photographs:
© David Churchill

Picture acknowledgements:
Pages 5, 17 (Charles Rennie Mackintosh portrait) © T&R Anna and Sons Ltd;
Pages 5 (sketch), 10, © Estudio Mariscal;
Pages 12, 14 (plan of building), 15 (delivery vans) © Hunterian Art Gallery;
Pages 14 (Mitchell Street façade), 15 (rotary presses), 18–19, 20–21, 24, 27 © Scottish Media Group;
Pages 30, 31 © Ozturk Modelmakers;
Pages 32–35 © Page and Park Architects

Series editor: Sarah Gaventa, Communications Director, Glasgow 1999
Editor: Nick Barley
Art director: Stephen Coates
Designer: Anne Odling-Smee
Copy editors: Jessica Lack, Alex Stetter
Editorial assistant: Jonathan Heaf

Contributors:
Stuart MacDonald
Alan Crawford
Ian Jack
Page and Park Architects
Texts © the authors

Production co-ordinated by:
Uwe Kraus GmbH
Printed in Italy by Musumeci

Previous page: A new life for The Lighthouse. Escalators carry visitors through a new atrium to a series of permanent and temporary exhibition spaces in Scotland's Centre for Architecture, Design and the City.

Preface

6

Deyan Sudjic

A beacon for Scotland

8

Stuart MacDonald, the first director of The Lighthouse, introduces the vision for Scotland's Centre for Architecture, Design and the City

Seeds of greatness

12

The Lighthouse was the first building designed by Charles Rennie Mackintosh. Alan Crawford traces the history of a landmark in Scottish architecture

Paper architecture

20

For almost 90 years, The Lighthouse building was home to the *Glasgow Herald*. Ian Jack remembers his time as a junior writer for the paper in the 1960s

New life for the building

30

Page and Park Architects have reinterpreted the building by adding a new structure. The architects shed light on the design strategy

Around The Lighthouse

36

A photographic account of the building as it is today

A wealth of things to do

62

A guide to the centre's facilities and resources

Preface

One of the key issues underpinning Glasgow's strategy for its year as UK City of Architecture and Design was the idea that 1999 was not an end in itself, but would have a permanent legacy. A legacy that would be both cultural and physical. The Lighthouse, Scotland's Centre for Architecture, Design and the City, represents both. It is one of the city's finest architectural landmarks, Charles Rennie Mackintosh's first major building, the former home of the *Glasgow Herald*, and back in use after almost 15 years of dereliction looking better than ever. In the course of the restoration, the architects Page and Park have given Glasgow its best piece of new architecture since the opening of The Burrell. And what was once a neglected corner of the city centre has been brought back to life.

But just as important as the physical fact of the building is what will happen inside it. Under the Lighthouse Trust, and with its own director and staff, The Lighthouse is a new institution for Scotland, the largest architecture and design centre in Europe, a place which is dedicated to the proposition that architecture, urbanism and design are essential parts of contemporary culture, with a programme that sets out to involve and excite the widest audience for the subject.

Achieving the successful opening of The Lighthouse by Her Majesty The Queen in July 1999 was the product of a great deal of work by many people. The original idea came from the Glasgow 1999: UK City of Architecture and Design steering committee. When I was appointed director of Glasgow 1999, the idea of restoring the old *Herald* building, its new purpose, and the name for the centre were already in place. The next step was to realise it. A strategy that involved Glasgow City Council acquiring the building on behalf of the project, allowing Glasgow 1999 to apply for grants and lottery funds, was drawn up. Eleanor McAllister was seconded to Glasgow 1999 to manage the project, and worked successfully with Historic Scotland, the European Regional Development Fund, the Heritage and Scottish Arts Council Lottery Funds and the Glasgow Development Agency to raise the capital, and to oversee the building process, helped by generous private sector sponsorship.

With its rooftop café, its new viewing gallery and its inviting entrance, there is nothing quite like The Lighthouse. It has a constituency that goes far beyond the professional world of architecture and design. It is a place in which schoolchildren are as comfortable as architects.

At the heart of Page and Park's conception of the conversion is the idea that the new building is focused both on Mackintosh's architecture, turning it literally into a living exhibit, and on Glasgow itself, as a unique city. In this they have succeeded brilliantly.

Deyan Sudjic is director of Glasgow 1999: UK City of Architecture and Design

The original building was erected in 1895 to house the *Glasgow Herald* and was Charles Rennie Mackintosh's first major project.

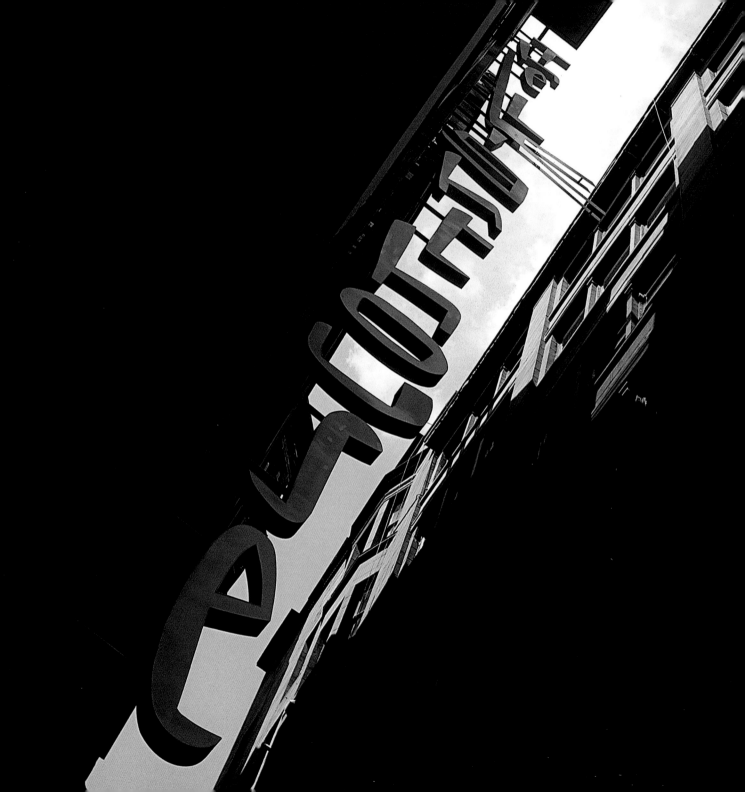

A beacon for Scotland

Reaching out and drawing in, The Lighthouse is a timely creation, given the current, popular interest in design matters. The opening of The Lighthouse as Scotland's Centre for Architecture, Design and the City is timely, not least because Enric Miralles' vision for the Edinburgh parliament building has captured the public imagination, opening up a debate about architecture, democracy and the nature of cultural identity. At the same time, the community is questioning the relationship between architects and clients, cities and citizenship and how we can negotiate the future.

With its mission to educate, to engage, to reach out and to innovate, The Lighthouse is particularly well placed to address the contemporary need to involve the public in issues to do with the built environment and mass-produced objects. The Lighthouse sees architecture and design as social, educational and economic concerns which are important to everyone.

Page and Park's conversion of The Lighthouse building facilitates that aspiration, superbly. The industrial toughness of the building translates well into flexible spaces for a range of purposes, such as education, exhibitions, conferences, Design into Business, a Charles Rennie Mackintosh interpretation centre, and facilities for cafés and a shop. Also, Page and Park's two new extensions, one, nicknamed the 'battery pack' which has created the entrance, circulation and additional exhibition space, the other called the 'Dow' after the building which was demolished to make way for office, store and workshop space, have added considerably to The Lighthouse's muscle in terms of access through the

Stuart MacDonald, the first director of The Lighthouse introduces the vision for Scotland's Centre for Architecture, Design and the City

building and additional smaller galleries.

The Lighthouse's development is a model of partnership with contributions from the Scottish Arts Council Lottery Fund, the National Heritage Lottery Fund, Historic Scotland, the European Regional Development Fund, The Glasgow Development Agency, Glasgow City Council and, not least, facilitation from the Glasgow 1999 Festival Company. This pulling together of resources towards a mutually agreed objective exemplifies the direction The Lighthouse might take in the future.

Debates about the value of architecture centres focus on the fact that architecture is physical and environmental; it is out there. Architecture cannot necessarily be experienced in the same way as fine art in a gallery. But The Lighthouse in itself offers an architectural experience. The way the Centre is sensed by visitors is a formative one. You enter through contemporary glass and steel, then ascend the building by escalator moving past traditional materials – sandstone, tiles and brick. The effect of the tactile surfaces making up the back of the

The entrance to The Lighthouse is in a new structure in Mitchell Lane (left). The competition to redevelop The Lighthouse building was won by Glasgow-based architects Page and Park.

10

Spanish designer Javier Mariscal was selected to create a graphic identity (below and right) for The Lighthouse after an international competition. His signage system (far right) is centred on a mast which ascends through the newly-built atrium. Mariscal was also responsible for the memorable Cobi symbol for the 1992 Barcelona Olympics.

Mackintosh building is strong and offers a brilliant contrast to the lightness of the newer materials of the "battery pack". This intimate sensation of the building's construction is even more forceful as you climb the original tower – the suspended staircase takes you into close contact with massive and roughly hewn sandstone blocks particularly as the tower corbells out. You become aware of the creative tension between the old and new, the sensuousness of the materials, stylistic differences, changes in building technology and the sheer physicality of the architecture.

This induction into the world of architecture through a physical experience is continued when visitors climb up into either the old tower or new viewing platform. Depending on their point of view, visitors can look out over the city Mackintosh and his Victorian and Edwardian peers helped to create. Alternatively, the history of architecture can

be enjoyed in rooftop microcosm from David Hamilton's classical Royal Exchange to Wyllie Shanks' Corbusier-like College of Building and Printing. As well as interpretative visitor materials relating to this built experience, The Lighthouse has also created a guide to its urban setting, highlighting the uniqueness of Glasgow's grid plan, and celebrating architectural achievements such as the Art Deco extravaganza of Burton's shop and Gillespie Kidd and Coia's copper-clad infill building at the entrance to Mitchell Lane.

The Lighthouse also offers novel virtual experiences – Strathclyde University's ABACUS computer model of the city and Glasgow School of Art's Digital Design Studio that describes Glasgow's industrial design heritage. Public engagement with architecture and design is expanded through the education centre – purpose-designed and one of the largest within any institution of its kind – which, with its range of spaces for children and adults, will allow visitors to play and learn creatively. It is in education and community outreach especially that The Lighthouse intends to break new ground, working with the public on design problems in the real world, building on the success of Glasgow 1999's education and community initiative programmes. This proactive policy of including people in design and architecture also applies to exhibitions. Apart from offering a wide range of exhibitions, the aim is to make them interactive, complementing them with workshops, lectures and other activities.

This sets the agenda for a number of interrelated themes – the learning city, the creative city, the connected city. Running through these themes is the recognition that people are the key resources in the sustainability of our cities. The Lighthouse will communicate this agenda outwards whilst respecting local needs, working with its partners both here in Scotland and abroad.

Stuart MacDonald is the director of The Lighthouse. He is a founder member of the Scottish Education Trust and was an advisor to Strathclyde Region's education services.

12

THE "HERALD" BUILDI
MITCHELL St GLA

The Lighthouse was the first building designed by Charles Rennie Mackintosh. Alan Crawford traces the history of a landmark in Scottish architecture

Mackintosh's famous ink-on-paper perspective drawing c.1893 (left). The large tower which still dominates the building (right) was designed to hold a water tank, big enough to put out a fire in the printing presses.

Seeds of greatness

It is hard to imagine The Lighthouse building as it used to be. The bones of the structure are still in place, six floors of workspace and a grid of columns and beams. But imagine them filled not with the bright light of late 20th century design and consumption, but with the grimier atmosphere of manufacturing: vast printing presses thundering in the basement, ranks of men seated at keyboards typing out the daily events while newspapers are bundled into delivery vans outside.

The Lighthouse building is part of a longer history which is that of the *Glasgow Herald*, first published in 1783 and one of the oldest surviving British newspapers (the *Scotsman* was only launched 34 years later in 1817). It was first published in and around Trongate appearing twice weekly. Then in 1855 the crippling tax on newspapers known as stamp duty was abolished, and prices fell from sixpence to about a penny. In the following decades, newspapers enjoyed a phase of spectacular growth, sustained by the spread of literacy and new technology (speedier presses, telegraphy and the railway network). In 1858 the paper moved to a larger space, St Vincent Place and became a daily publication the following year.

But with the continuing pressures on production, the *Glasgow Herald* was obliged to buy land in Buchanan Street and over the next thirty years the paper carried out three building campaigns. In 1867 John Baird was invited to design a place to house the presses and other equipment and in 1879 James Sellars constructed a suitably imposing frontage (which now survives as 69 Buchanan Street). The

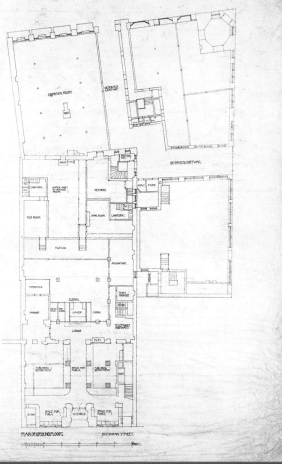

THE GLASGOW
HERALD BUILDINGS

PLAN OF GROUND FLOOR.   BUCHANAN STREET.

The *Glasgow Herald* was published at The Lighthouse building from 1899 until as late as 1980. Delivery vans drove into the building through a cobbled passageway off Mitchell Street (shown at the top of the plan, above) and collected newspapers from the despatch room on the ground floor.

The 150-foot water tower has an Ogee roof (right) and an art nouveau style that emphasises its scale.

The public entrance to the *Glasgow Herald* offices was through a building situated in Buchanan Street (above) which is today no longer connected to The Lighthouse. On the western side of the building in Mitchell Street (below right), delivery vans queued to collect papers as they rolled off the huge rotary presses in the basement.

third and final phase began fourteen years later, in 1893, and was spearheaded by the general manager Alexander Sinclair. Writing in his memoirs *Fifty Years of Newspaper Life: 1845–1895*, he explained that the greatest fear for a newspaper building was fire. He set about devising a system of sprinklers for both the inside and the outside of the *Glasgow Herald*'s offices. But this did not prevent the danger from fires in neighbouring properties and after a building nearby burnt down he resolved to buy up the land around the building.

The architects John Honeyman and John Keppie were invited to build what is now known as The Lighthouse and restructure the rest of the property at a cost of about £30,000. Keppie had, at one time, been James Sellars' chief assistant and it must have been with a certain amount of bravado that he set about to better his mentor's work. The designer on the project was the young Charles Rennie Mackintosh. The architects' relationship with the building was transitional. Keppie was seen as the initiator of the project, Honeyman explored the forms and functions of the building while Mackintosh contributed to the tower's image and was responsible for the famous perspective drawing (page 12). When The Lighthouse building was completed in 1895, it contained a stationary steam engine in the basement to drive the presses; a newspaper despatch room on the ground floor, with a cartway running past it; and an 8,000 gallon water tank at the top of the building's tower to supply half

of the paper's sprinklers. The rest was standard warehousing space inhabited by warehousemen, jobbing printers and commission agents. By 1899 there were presses in the basement of the building, and the editorial department of the *Glasgow Herald*'s sister paper, the *Evening Times*, was installed on one of the upper floors.

Built according to the latest structural methods, The Lighthouse building had external walls of load bearing masonry and an internal frame of cast iron columns, rolled steel beams and rolled iron joists. The direction of the principal beams changes from floor to floor; allowing for movement in the structure, and also, in case of fire, for it to pull two ways, helping to prevent the external walls from being pushed out. The roof structure consisted of steel beams linked by ball joints and stiffened by tie rods which allowed movement and helped 'true' columns made unsteady by fire.

Given the specialist nature of the construction, it is unlikely that the building was entirely designed by Mackintosh. The elevations however are certainly his. Six floors on the Mitchell Street elevation are in an orderly arrangement, with gabled bays at either end and a cornice above the third floor. The windows are detailed differently on each floor, but the treatment is kept plain until it reaches the dormers. This was the eclectic style of late Victorian commercial architecture, with echoes of Scottish tower houses in the upper floors.

The water tower stands alongside the main block like some great stiff-stalked flower. Mitchell Street is narrow, and Mackintosh did not design the tower to be seen from close up. From a distance, the tower can be seen to rise powerfully above the city, while from pavement level, it floats benignly overhead, its great height foreshortened. Its beauty (and originality) is in the mouldings and decorative details. Mackintosh used familiar historical motifs – here, the decorative shields held by putti (cherubs) in Renaissance decoration are elongated into warped hybrids that resemble elephants trunks. (The best view of the detail of the upper storeys is from the top of the multi-storey car park opposite.)

From about 1894–1899, in the later stages of Sinclair's 'Fear of Fire' campaign, other work was carried out; a four storey development was erected on the south side of the property, east of The Lighthouse; and Sellars' building was rearranged and redecorated. Mackintosh had a hand in redesigning the manager's office.

These building campaigns created a property that endured for much of the 20th century (the water tower was even used as a fire-watch post in the Second World War). The newspaper continued to be printed by the methods, if not the actual machines, of the 1890s until the introduction of desktop publishing. In London this meant escape from outdated labour relations and, after 1986, from Fleet Street. Likewise in Glasgow. The *Glasgow Herald*, by then owned by the multinational company Lonrho, bought premises in nearby Albion Street. The last hot-metal issue of the *Glasgow Herald* came out of The Lighthouse on Saturday 19 July 1980.

After the *Glasgow Herald* left, The Lighthouse remained empty. The whole *Herald* site, reaching to Buchanan Street, was acquired for development by Scottish Widows. But The Lighthouse did not form part of the plan. Eventually its conversion into a centre for architecture and design was proposed as an essential part of the Glasgow 1999 programme. The middle of the site was cleared of buildings, and a competition to adapt The Lighthouse was won by the Glasgow architects Page and Park. They designed a system of access and circulation which could be fitted to the exposed back of the building without disturbing the original structure. This created vertical, light-filled vistas to draw visitors towards the upper floors.

The architects saw Mackintosh's design as a plant rising to a blooming flower. Their work sensitively circles around the original chimneystack based at the back of the building, curving into The Lighthouse and out again, linking the old and the new, the past and the future.

Alan Crawford is a freelance historian and writer. He was the consultant for the Mackintosh Interpretation Centre at The Lighthouse.

Charles Rennie Mackintosh

1868 Charles Rennie Mackintosh was born in Glasgow on 7 June 1868

1883–1892 Studied at the Glasgow School of Art. Whilst there, Mackintosh met Margaret and Frances Macdonald and the artist Herbert MacNair. The four artists collaborated on designs for furniture, metalwork and illustration. Their style earned them the nickname the 'Spook School'. He began his career as an architect with the firm Honeyman and Keppie.

1893 At 25 he received his first major job – to design The Lighthouse building for the *Glasgow Herald*.

1896 Mackintosh won a competition to design the Glasgow School of Art. Work commenced in 1897 and continued until 1909. It was to be Mackintosh's finest achievement. During this period he designed a series of tea room interiors and built two large houses, Windyhill in Kilmacolm and The Hill House in Helensburgh.

1900 Contributed to the design of the 8th Vienna Secession. This was considered so successful that he was commissioned to build the Wamdorfer Music Salon. It was about this time that he married his long time collaborator Margaret Macdonald.

1902 Designed the Mackintosh Room at the Turin International Exhibition. While a partner with Honeyman and Keppie he completed a series of major projects in Glasgow including Queens Cross Church (1899) and the Scotland Street School (1906).

1914 By now Mackintosh was in poor health and suffering from depression. He moved to Walberswick in Suffolk. There he started to paint flowers for a book to be printed in Germany. His supposedly suspect behavior, walking alone on beaches, making drawings and drinking alone in the village pub, led to his appearance before a magistrate accused of being a German spy.

1915 The couple moved to London, where Mackintosh resumed his architectural practice. He produced designs for the 'Dug Out' tea room in Glasgow and the interiors of Bassett-Lowke's house in Northampton. These designs, of primary colours and geometric motifs represented a new direction in his work.

1923 The Mackintoshes left London and moved to the South of France where Mackintosh gave up architecture altogether and devoted himself to painting landscapes.

1928 Mackintosh died in London in virtual obscurity.

Compositors (previous pages) were responsible for setting hot-metal type, using special keyboards. In 1965, when the *Glasgow Herald* employed over 1,000 people, it was considered strictly men's work. After The Lighthouse was vacated by the newspaper in 1980, it stood empty and derelict for over 15 years (left).

In 1965, when I was aged twenty, I got a job on the *Glasgow Herald* as a trainee journalist. My final interview was with the editor in the Buchanan Street building. What I remember of this meeting is the severity of the editor's secretary, Miss Frost, a tall woman in her sixties with her hair in a bun, and the contrasting shyness of the editor himself, Alastair Warren. As I was also shy – and at this point anxious – the room must have been filled with polite Scottish hesitation. Warren, who was related to a prominent Glasgow business dynasty, wore the kind of dark suit I'd seen on brokers leaving the Glasgow Stock Exchange, a few hundred yards up Buchanan Street. Not a suit that came from Burton's, or Hepworth's, or (like mine) from Jackson's The Tailor in Sauchiehall Street. I noticed – something that gave me a little confidence – a dusting of dandruff which had gathered, unusually, on the trouser-leg. When it came to be my turn for questions, the editor having run out of his own, I remember asking what a journalist could expect to earn, eventually.

The editor said: "Oh, if you do very well then I think

For almost 90 years,
The Lighthouse
was home to the
Glasgow Herald.
Ian Jack remembers
his time as a junior
writer at the paper
in the 1960s

Paper architecture

you could expect as much as £2,000 a year by the time you're 30."

In the meantime the salary would be £400. I would be trained in sub-editing in the subs' room and in reporting in the newsroom, and then, after a few months, I'd be sent to a local weekly (Hugh Fraser, the store magnate, had bought several as a job lot in his recent acquisition of the company which published the *Glasgow Herald* and its sister daily, the *Evening Times*). There this training would be put into practice and my salary would rise to £600. But first I was to start in the features department. That was our first and last conversation. Miss Frost showed me out.

Some weeks later, having worked out my notice at Motherwell Public Library, I turned up in the features room, which was small and dark and contained exotic people: a young woman in a fur coat and gold-rimmed spectacles; a young man in shirtsleeves who spoke through a fag in his mouth. Galley-proofs and the tools of sub-editing lay scattered across a few desks: metal spikes for discarded copy, scissors, glue pots, ashtrays, teacups, and a special ruler which measured type and which I learned to call an 'em-stick'.

'Features' were a relatively new idea on the paper, which was powered by the engines of news and commercial information, and the people who generated 'feature articles' were regarded by the rest, I think, as workers at the trivial, luxury end of the trade. To me, they were kind and encouraging. Praise was not then common parlance in the Scottish workplace, or none that I'd worked in, and here people seemed to praise each other all the time. 'Great piece this

Alastair Warren (above) editor of the *Glasgow Herald* in 1965. His office was in a separate part of the building from the printing and finishing machinery.

morning, Willie... good headline, Jim... nice caption, Lesley.' Most of this came from the features editor, David Hogarth, the man with the Players Gold Leaf in his mouth. Under his kind eye, I took my first steps in the trade and began to find my way about the place.

For anyone who had a romantic view of newspapers, as I had, the building seemed back to front. Profit was ranked above journalism. The accounting and advertising departments monopolised the frontage on Buchanan Street; here, in a hall lined with desks, quaintly called 'the counting house', members of the public paid cash for their small ads and staff wages were stuffed into brown envelopes. Editorial and publishing staff, on the other hand, usually came and went through the side entrance (like a stage door) in Mitchell Lane, which stayed open all hours. A lift (known as the 'hoist') ran from here to every floor. The basement held the rotary presses and newsprint rolls. The top storey, which had windows in the roof, was occupied by the composing room; compositors needed light. Separating these two stages of the industrial process lay the editorial floors of the *Herald* and the *Evening Times* (and, until 1961, also of a fondly-remembered little daily called the *Bulletin* (Scottish Nationalist in sentiment and, perhaps, ahead of its time).

Within the editorial floors, the geography was complicated. Wayward corridors connected rooms: separate rooms for features, for the library, for reporters, sub-editors, leader-writers, the women's page, the diary column ('From All Quarters', this title surmounted by a small drawing of a weathervane), the commercial and business pages, even a room for the paper's two shipbuilding correspondents and another reporter who was confined to coverage of coal and steel. All of these rooms had the same smell, a compound of cigarette smoke, hot lead, etching acid, machine oil and newsprint, though closer to the canteen it gave way to hot fat and gravy. There were the obvious noises – typewriters, telephones – but in the composing room you heard the tinkling slither of lead newly-cast by Linotype machines, and in the hushed subs' room the hiss of air into the pneumatic tubes which delivered edited copy to the compositors.

From the process department, where half-tone plates were mounted on steel blocks, came the screech of power-saws cutting mounts to the right dimensions. Outside at the back in Mitchell Street, newspaper vans honked and manoeuvred through most of the day and quite a lot of the night.

With more than a thousand others, I worked in a factory.

I learned factory habits. When the job was done, and the first edition had caught its trains to Inverness and London, we went for a drink in one of two factory pubs. The Gordon Arms (now Ross's) in Mitchell Lane catered for the more effete, the features people and one or two stray civilians who had forgotten to go home from their jobs in building societies. Sammy Dow's, round the corner in Mitchell Street (where Page and Park's new extension now stands) was for printers and hardened sub-editors and reporters, men who had sometimes served in convoys and destroyers in the war, Senior Service types who had no truck with filter-tips. I never dared go into Dow's, but the pattern of drinking in Ross's was much the same. Men stood each other rounds of beer and whiskey. Women were a rarity. After six o'clock the only women to be found in the building among the hundreds of men were the couple who ran the women's page, the canteen ladies, and Marie in the library.

Once, when we found ourselves together in the composing room, the women's page editor's assistant looked at the ranks of men seated in front of their Linotype keyboards and remarked to me that here was a job that could be done just as well, if not better, by women.

It was an astonishing thought.

The *Glasgow Herald* at that time was a classic British broadsheet newspaper. It was ancient (founded in 1783, two years before *The Times*); it had replaced advertising with news on its front page only seven years before; it had a London office – a handsome building on Fleet Street – which sent City and political news by teleprinter, and (once a week) a 'London Letter' which described social and cultural aspects of the capital. It took itself seriously as Britain's leading newspaper outside those published

from London. Its rival, the *Scotsman*, also posted such claims, but the *Scotsman* had a smaller circulation (and in any case came out of Edinburgh, which Glasgow recognised as a capital, but only in the Canberra-Pretoria-Brasilia sense of the word – as an unreal place of no other account). It saw its most important audience as the Glasgow business community. It was imperturbably sober, politically and socially conservative and made few concessions, apart from the football reports, to the popular culture of the city or the nation. Razor gangs, music-hall comedians, domestic murder, Lulu – all these well-known features of Glasgow life were covered more enthusiastically by the city's other titles: by the *Evening Times* in the same building, by the *Daily Record* and the *Sunday Mail* a few blocks to the west in Hope Street, by the *Sunday Post* to the north in Port Dundas, and by the *Scottish Daily Express* and the *Evening Citizen* to the east in their black-glass building in Albion Street. Several other great industrial and commercial cities had once had papers like the *Glasgow Herald* – the *Liverpool Echo*, the *Birmingham Post*, the *Manchester Guardian*, the *Yorkshire Post* in Leeds – but by the 1960s most had begun to adjust their sights to a more popular local audience, or, in the *Guardian*'s case, ditched provincialism for a metropolitan identity by moving head office to London. Glasgow in 1965 was no longer the second city of the Empire or even of Britain – its population had been overtaken in size by Birmingham's in 1951 – but it retained an importance

and a self-regard which was reflected by its most serious newspaper and the only one to carry the word Glasgow in its title.

All this was about to change, but in 1965 it was impossible to know how soon or by how much. Tenements were being demolished and replaced by tower blocks; new housing estates had grown on the outskirts; the trams had gone in 1962 (the last run prompted the biggest crowds in the streets since VE day; Glasgow had a peculiar fondness for trams). But at its centre, the face and structure of the city would still have been recognisable to a Victorian.

This had its drawbacks. A mile or so from the *Herald*'s office, my best friend still lived in a room and kitchen in a Cowcaddens tenement with his mother and grandmother, where they shared a lavatory with a neighbouring flat on the same landing and where washing (other than in the kitchen sink) could be accomplished only by walking with a towel to the public baths. But to nostalgists with bathrooms, Glasgow offered treats. On summer mornings you could still take an excursion steamer down the river from a wharf in the city centre. From other wharves close by, cross-channel packets left nightly for Belfast and ships of the Anchor Line still sailed with passengers for Bombay. Large railway termini – Glasgow was remarkably endowed with four of them – still stood at either end of Buchanan Street. Steam and smoke from locomotives heading commuter trains to Wemyss Bay and East Kilbride drifted through the fretwork of the bridges across the Clyde.

Such things by 1965, I guess, had begun to look not long for this world. Other everyday ways of Glasgow living seemed more permanent. Buses the colours of the Irish tricolour carried the Glasgow coat of arms on their sides together with the name of the man who managed the fleet – E.R.L. Fitzpayne (a name more familiar to Glaswegians than the signature on the Bank of England's notes). Indian restaurants had sprung up near the university, but other than in those and high-tea tearooms, Glasgow ate out only on special occasions in restaurants which held terrors of formality for the customers who had saved up to eat in them (Ferrari's in Sauchiehall Street, the

Rogano, still a favourite with Glaswegians today, is a reminder of Glasgow's glamourous metropolitan qualities, and the days when eating out was reserved for very special occasions.

© SCOTTISH MEDIA GROUP

Sammy Dow's Pub in Mitchell Street (above) was for printers, hardened sub-editors and reporters – unlike The Gordon Arms in Mitchell Lane, where the features people drank. Today, Sammy Dow's has been replaced with a new extension to The Lighthouse.

Malmaison in the Central Hotel, the Rogano just off Exchange Square). No pubs – or none that I knew of – sold wine other than the fortified sherry-like stuff which marked out the impoverished and desperate drinker. On Saturday afternoons, Glaswegians shopped at department stores with names which were unique to the city; Pettigrew and Stephen, Copeland and Lye, Treron et Cie, Arnott Simpson, Inglis, MacDonald, Wylie and Lochhead, Paisley's. On Saturday nights, they went to theatres (five of them), a great concentration of cinemas (Green's in Renfield Street was reputedly the largest in Europe), and dance halls (the Locarno, Majestic, Plaza, Dennistoun Palais, Barrowland and Albert) where bouncers sniffed at the men in the queue of the more elite establishments and refused admission to anyone smelling too yeastily of drink. On Sundays, save for the Kelvingrove Museum and Art Gallery (and the occasional hotel bar with a generously interpreted liquor license for 'bona fide travellers'), the city was shut. The old weekly cycle continued; five days for work, the sixth for enjoyment, the seventh for reflection, reverence, self-recrimination, and recovery.

It was a singular way of living, sentimentalised even then but not yet folkloric – real to those who lived it. The city's economy had been slowly shrinking since the start of the century; the latest cull of its industry had occurred a few years earlier in the 1960s with the closure of the North British Locomotive Company and a scattering of Clyde shipyards, Blythswood, Henderson, Denny's at Dumbarton. A skyline of chimneys and cranes had taken a thinning. But Glasgow was still smoke-blackened and its remaining sources of wealth still obvious. The eastern suburbs lived under the haze of Lanarkshire's steel smelters, rolling mills, steel plate and tube manufacturers. Downriver, to the west, welders' torches sparked from hulls on the slipways of Fairfield, Alexander Stephen, Connel's, Yarrow's, Barclay Curle, Fleming and Ferguson. At John Brown's yard in Clydebank, they had just laid the keel for the QE2. Further off, in Greenock, Lithgows had ambitious plans to build supertankers and ore-carriers.

Change was coming – I think we could see that.

The city was drawing up plans for a motorway which would cut through its heart. Architects' illustrations and models showed curving roads dotted with a few speeding cars and bordered by saplings, grassland and tower blocks. There was a pure blind confidence about these plans and they met little resistance. In a city where the past meant the kind of slum my best friend still lived in, ideas of 'conservation' had little appeal. It was easy to reduce the city's rich 19th century legacy to the narrower and more desperate facts of cramped and rotten housing stock.

Where was the architecture of Rennie Mackintosh and Greek Thomson in all this? In the popular imagination, nowhere. In the *Glasgow Herald*'s offices, a few keen students of the city's history knew Mackintosh had designed the tower on the Mitchell Street corner, where the paper's drama critic, Christopher Small, hammered at his typewriter composing reviews. But I think it would be fair to say that, to most people who worked in his building, Mackintosh meant another Glasgow man who invented a handier Glasgow style, the raincoat.

The *Glasgow Herald* no longer employs shipbuilding correspondents and is now called the *Herald* – an attempt to broaden its appeal beyond the city and its western hinterland. That tells its own story. Much of the power and influence in Scottish life has switched from the west to the east. The Forth is now a busier river than the Clyde, Edinburgh fast reaching the same size as Glasgow.

It is still a fine and interesting city, better in many ways – though not for everybody who lives in it – than the one I knew 35 years ago, made cleaner and lighter by its switch from production to consumption, from the factory to the shop. Still, I think I was lucky to catch the final years of its largest historical purpose, when the vocabulary of its achievement could still be spoken in the present tense, and was thick with names (Barclay Curle, Pettigrew and Stephen) other than those of its best architects.

Ian Jack is editor of Granta *magazine. He started his career at the* Glasgow Herald *and then went on to work at the* Sunday Times *and as editor of the* Independent on Sunday.

The Lighthouse is situated at the edge of the Glasgow urban grid, where the bend in Mitchell Street allows the elaborate corner water tower to be seen soaring way above the rooftops. This is the focal point of the grade A listed Charles Rennie Mackintosh building, which along with our recent additions, forms The Lighthouse. The small doorway at this corner, seen in the flamboyant Mackintosh drawing (see page 12), only gave access to a part of the ground floor, while the main approach to the building was half way along Mitchell Street, but both these doorways were too small to provide a suitable entrance for The Lighthouse.

The new extension we have designed at the rear, with a frontage on to Mitchell Lane, allows space for a generous entrance, as well as providing the required easy public access to all floor levels with minimal interference with the old building. This new structure is only attached to the old building where necessary, and the gap between them is closed by glass. It contains the large entrance and foyer area (where Javier Mariscal's signage pole stands) with escalators, lifts and stairs. The original doors at the base of the corner tower and on Mitchell Street give access only to the ground floor and basement. We have added a further new building on Mitchell Street to provide administration offices and storage. In contrast to the Mitchell Lane entrance which is open and welcoming, using glass, stone, timber and copper, the façade to the new extension on Mitchell Street is closed and private, with its lead shutters and large aluminium adjustable louvres.

The Lighthouse accommodation begins on the first floor with a warehouse-style exhibition space, as the basement and ground floor accommodate units for commercial rent. The second floor is devoted to education and children and the third contains the Charles Rennie Mackintosh Interpretation Centre and a conference suite. The fourth and fifth floors contain exhibition galleries and a stylish rooftop café. All these functions which can change if necessary are contained within the old building, with each floor spilling out onto the new extension. It is now possible for the public to climb the old corner water tower, as

Page and Park's challenge was to retain the spirit of the original design, while improving circulation around the building and allowing each floor to function autonomously. The model was built by Ozturk Models.

Page and Park Architects have reinterpreted the building by adding a new structure. Here, they shed light on the thinking behind the design

New life for the building

32

Each of the five floors could be interpreted to represent a chronological step in the seasonal transformation of a flower:

1. The circular elaboration above the doorway on Mitchell Street represents a flower's bulb. Above this on the first and second floors are two plain windows. The second has an extended cill. This represents the forming of roots.

2. Further up on the third floor the top of the window extends and develops an unusual split pediment head and a semicircular ring. This is the flower emerging.

3. On the fourth floor the semicircular ring thickens and the cill extends further out. The flower has formed.

4. At the fifth floor the semi-circular ring thins slightly. The flower is begining to wilt.

5. Slightly below the fifth floor are a number of arched windows. They correspond to the mature flower, complete with its central stigma.

6. A more flamboyant version of the mature flower is in a window adjacent to the water tower. This corresponds to the flower ageing and spreading its petals. As a pre-futurist expression the frontage on Mitchell Street seeks to catch two moments in time in one pictorial image.

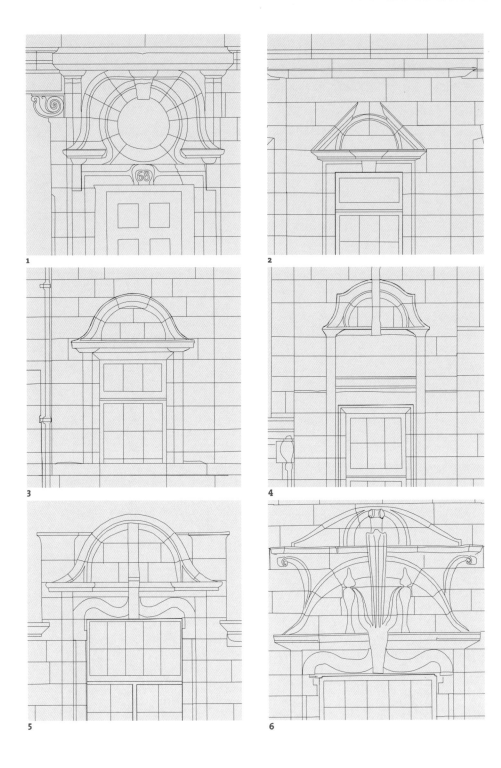

1

2

3

4

5

6

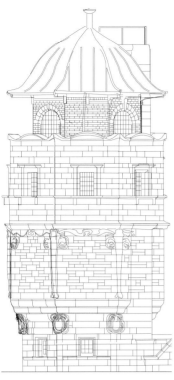

The water tower can be seen as a flower-head with the chimney stack behind as the seed-pod. It was with this botanical symbolism in mind that architects Page and Park formed the new structure in four parts. At the lowest levels the swelling of the ground floor entrance is generated from a radius extended from the 'seed-pod' chimney, while at the middle levels the radius shapes the 'stalk' through which the visitor climbs towards the light above.

The flowering metaphor is echoed in the upper floors by at fourth, the large panels of metal cladding, glass and stone, with the artwork sliding shutter in front, with above it at fifth the openness of the free floating balcony 'hen run'. Ultimately the new tower emerges above all this, envisaged as a fragment of the initial radial geometry, accessible to all via the passenger lift.
The restoration has resulted in the creation of a new east façade (below).

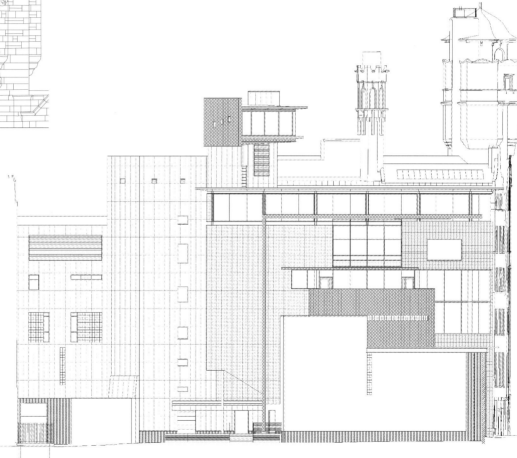

The plan of the restored building (right) demonstrates the new circulation space described by the architects as the 'battery pack', situated at the bottom of the drawing. Its construction meant that the large rooms within the old building would not have to be filled with new staircases and lifts. The water tower, however, (seen at the top right of the plan) would form the perfect location for a set-piece helical staircase.

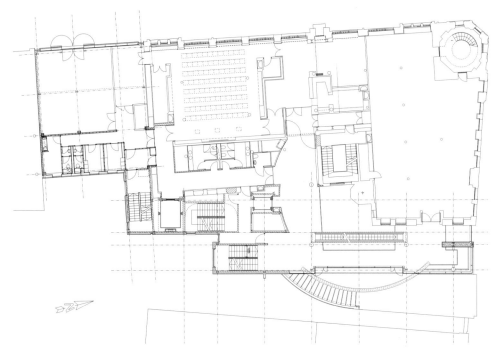

we have carved out the floors and water tank and suspended from the roof a new helical steel and timber access stair. The subsequent connection between this stair and the main circulation was made by the designer of the Mackintosh Interpretation Centre, Gareth Hoskins.

Mitchell Lane represents the city of Glasgow at its densest, with towering office buildings which seem to squeeze its vertical volume, making the space almost unbearable. The Lighthouse extension enables the lane to breathe, opening it out at the entrance and using the circulation flow up the escalators and lifts to the top daylit roof as the visitor climbs up the side of the old building. A new viewing tower rises up alongside the old water tower and chimney stack , providing access for all to panoramic views of the existing building and the city centre.

In the early stages of The Lighthouse design competition, the artist Jack Sloan suggested that the original building design was permeated by an intricate botanical symbolism. It could be read as a bluebell, growing from a seedling on the ground floor facade into a spirited organic flowering at the top. At an imaginative level, this structure of seedling, emergence, flowering and dispersal can be said to anticipate the role of the new centre, which embraces both examination and incubation of urban and design concepts as well as presentation and dissemination to a wider world. It seems appropriate that the new tower should have found birth in the wish of Deyan Sudjic to create an accessible viewing point above the city rooflines. Like a Geddesian outlook tower, it confirms the Glasgow dream of building a vehicle to look into the future to anticipate, challenge and promote design. This tower rises out above the stone plinth of the city to look beyond its boundaries, limits and restrictions, yet at the same time it confirms existing values and essences.

Page & Park Architects were formed in 1981. The firm has established a reputation for innovative new architecture and sensitive restoration.

After a two year restoration project, The Lighthouse opened to the public in July 1999 as a high point in Glasgow's year as UK City of Architecture and Design. It was fitting that the inaugural exhibition at Scotland's Centre for Architecture, Design and the City featured the work of another of Glasgow's great architectural heroes, Alexander 'Greek' Thomson. This series of photographs illustrates the variety of activities taking place at The Lighthouse, as well as providing a record of the restoration which has brought new life to Charles Rennie Mackintosh's first building.

Around The Lighthouse

Photography by
Philip Sayer
and David Churchill

One of two new extensions to
the building, the copper-clad
'battery pack' (left), houses
the service and access
facilities for the building.
Its escalators and staircases
lead up to a viewing
platform which offers a new
outlook over the city skyline.

Respecting the historical importance of the Mackintosh building is a key part of the restoration, and the original Mitchell Street façade (left) has remained largely untouched. The only sign of the radical changes inside is the new Dow extension, whose private-looking façade is in contrast to the public entrance around the corner in Mitchell Lane (right), where Javier Mariscal's suspended signage is highly visible from Buchanan Street.

Inside the building, visitors enter a vast light-filled atrium space which allows views up to the top floor. A staircase sweeps up around the copper-clad interior wall, while escalators climb the full height of the atrium, offering a vertiginous ascent.

A changing selection of work by young designers is on show in the Review Gallery (left). This display showcases products by Spanish design group El Ultimo Grito

In the refurbished original building at first floor level, a large temporary exhibition space (above) accommodates international touring shows such as Philippe Starck's 'Vanity Case'.

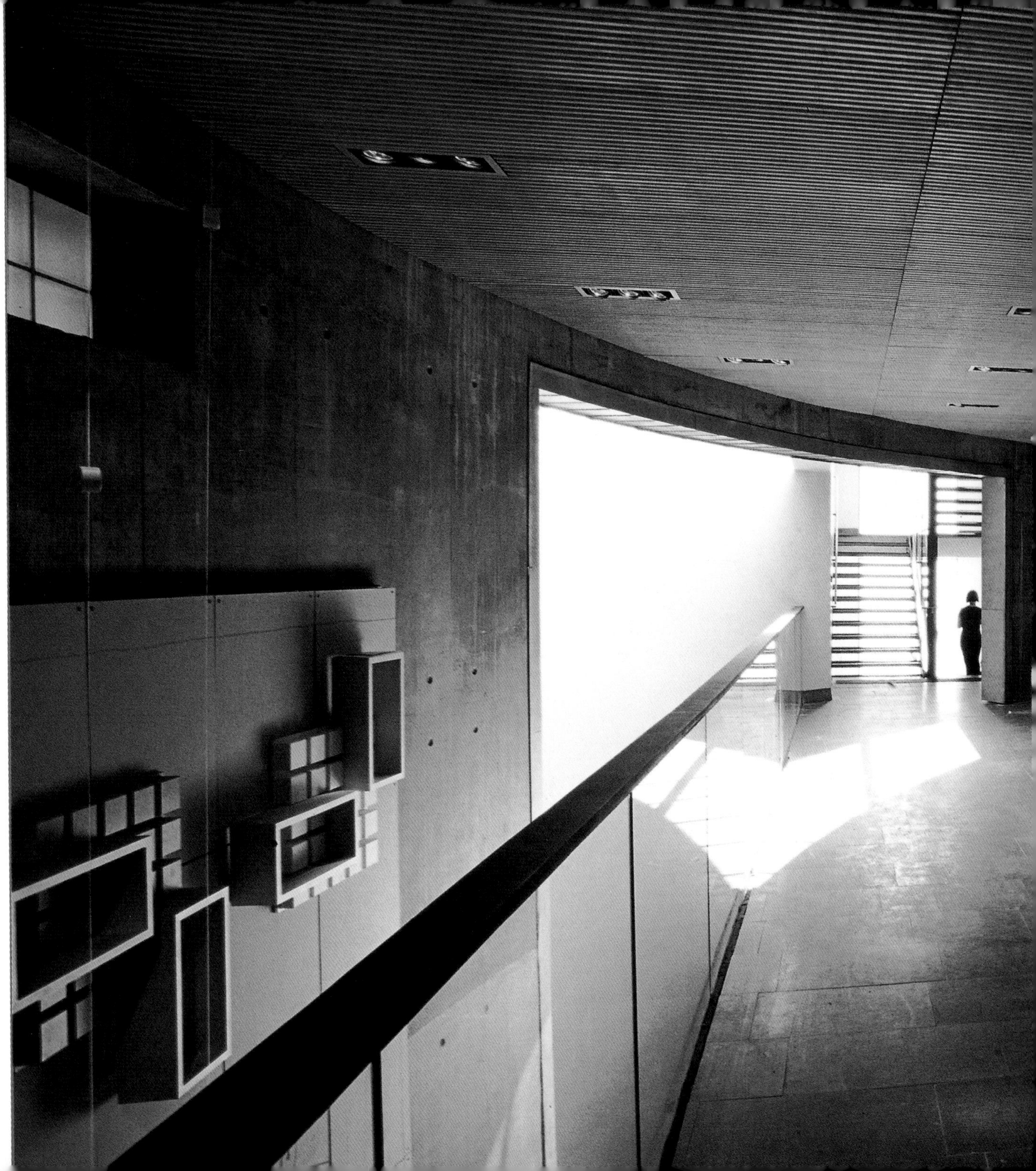

Climbing upwards from first floor level to the Doocot café at the top, the staircase is built around Alexander Beleschenko's artwork in etched blue glass (left). The Mackintosh Interpretation Centre (overleaf) is situated on the third floor.

The main temporary exhibition spaces are located on the fifth and sixth floors, where the steel tie-rods of the Mackintosh roof remain visible. A model of Alexander 'Greek' Thomson's Queens Park Church centre (right), by the model making firm Telford, is shown in The Lighthouse's inaugural exhibition.

It was originally designed to house an enormous water tank large enough to dispel fears about the risk of fire in the *Glasgow Herald*'s printing presses. Today the water tower's tank has been removed and a helical staircase inserted in its place, leading to a small viewing platform at the top.

Looking down into the atrium from fifth floor level (left), the marriage of new and old materials is clearly visible. Overhead, through the glass roof, a Mackintosh tower can be seen beside Page and Park's viewing platform.

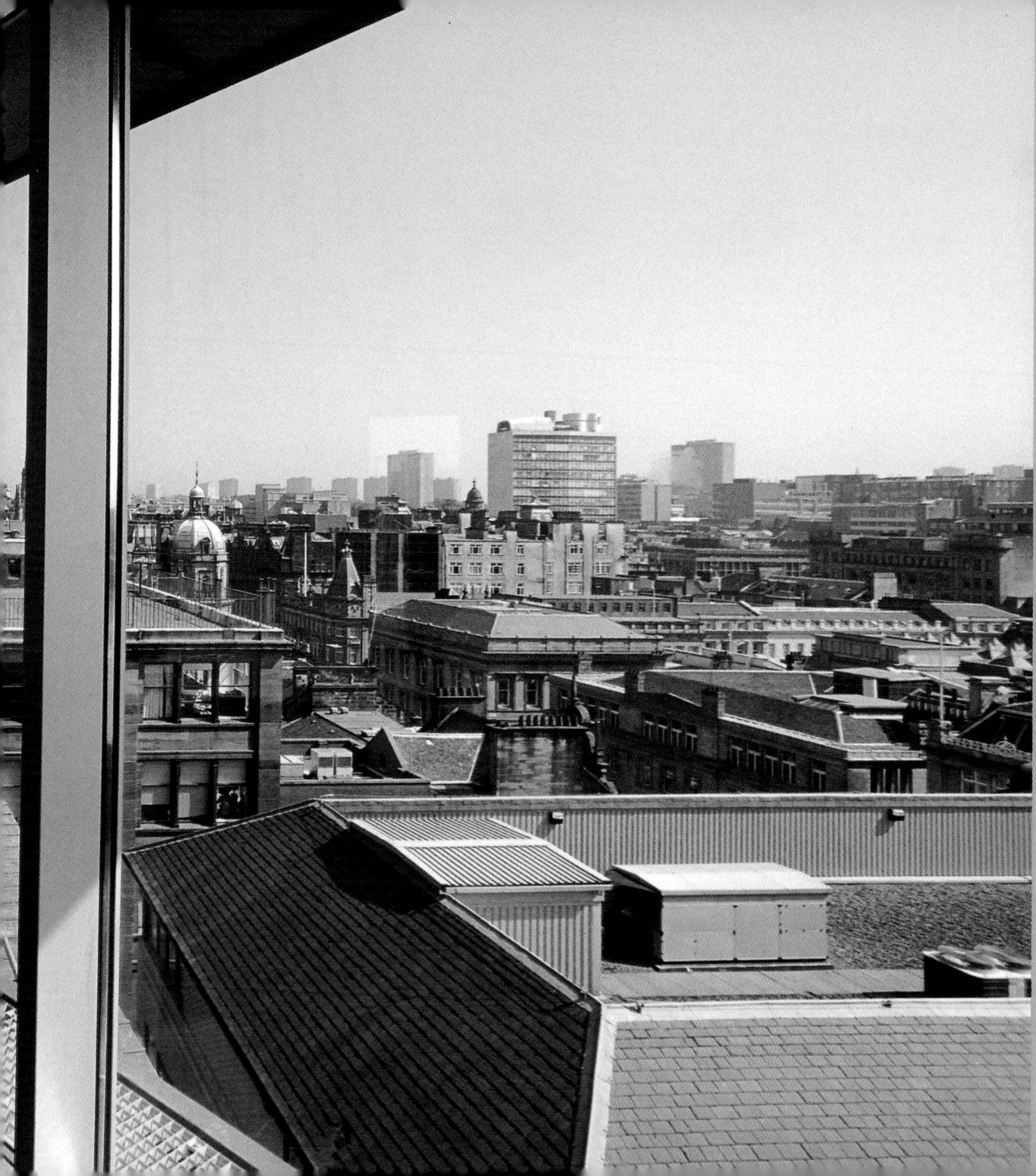

Mackintosh Interpretation Centre
The Mackintosh Centre is the facility dedicated to the study of the work of architect Charles Rennie Mackintosh. Designed by Gareth Hoskins, it plays a leading role in The Lighthouse's education strategy as an innovative, interactive learning resource for people of all ages and all levels of experience. Highlights include access to The Lighthouse water tower designed by Mackintosh, giving stunning views over the city. In addition to the facilities within the centre there is a programme of events throughout the year, focusing on specific themes such as Mackintosh and chair design. The programme includes seminars, lectures, workshops, study days, gallery tours and visits to other Mackintosh buildings in and around Glasgow.

Tickets: Adults £2.50; Children £1.50; Concessions £2.00; School Groups FREE. Schools should book through the Education Centre.

Temporary exhibitions
There are four main temporary exhibition galleries, a review gallery and one permanent exhibition space. The Lighthouse runs a programme of exhibitions throughout the year, on themes related to architecture, design and the city. The entire second floor is dedicated to education.

The Young Designers Gallery
A varied programme of exhibitions which highlight projects produced at The Lighthouse, as well as those undertaken as part of local, national and international outreach initiatives.

The Glass Box
A resource room showcasing new products and containing a range of design objects which will form a handling collection. Displays change in response to the issues raised by temporary exhibitions and education projects.

Wee People's City
An interactive play environment on the theme of building and the city. Aimed at children aged between 3 and 8 years, it promotes active learning, investigation, exploration, imagination, discovery and fun. Designed by Zoo Architects, the Wee People's City has been divided into two distinct areas – a busy play area and a quiet 'chill out' space. The busy interactive area is based on a city, and uses the particularities of the Glasgow

The Mackintosh Centre (right) is a permanent facility dedicated to the study of Mackintosh's art. It runs an events programme focusing on Mackintosh and the city of Glasgow.

The Doocot café on the fifth floor (right) is designed by the Glasgow firm Graven Images. Wee People's City (below), an interactive play space designed by Zoo Architects, uses computer animation as well as more traditional educational tools.

cityscape as its inspiration. Geometric street plans, rail and river networks are incorporated into contoured rubber flooring. Models of city buildings include an airport and railway station which are illuminated by under-floor fibre optic lighting. A range of building blocks encourages children to learn about scale, buildings and urban design and a three metre tower allows them to climb up for a bird's eye view of the cityscape beneath. Other elements include an A–Z of building materials; an underground system and a multi-denominational church with different roof designs to choose from. The highlight of the quiet 'chill out' space is a fantastic virtual 'fly through' computer animation by Robot which is projected onto a ceiling-mounted screen. Children can lie back on soft furniture to watch a journey through the animated cityscape which is populated by car-driving rabbits, planes and underground trains.

The Review Gallery

The Review Gallery is located on the mezzanine level of the first floor of the circulation space. Located in the extension to the Mackintosh building it has views through to the double height foyer space and to the central void. The exhibition system has been designed by lwd; Glasgow-based designers who have been working with Javier Mariscal on the internal design and graphics for

the building. The Review Gallery previews the work of designers who are seen to have caught the trends of the moment, are innovative in their approach and who are about to break into a wider market. The exhibition may focus on their wider practice or on a single item of design, exposing the process that has led to the prototype or finished product. This will include the conceptual side of their practice as well as an explanation as to how the product is made. The gallery's aims are:
● To provide a platform for the work of young and innovative designers
● To highlight the latest prototypes
● To present conceptual and practical disciplines
● To review current trends

The Workshop

A large flexible space for workshops, seminars and training sessions. Resources include books, journals, CD-Roms and videos

covering architecture, design, the arts, the urban environment and contemporary living.

IT Hotspot

A centre for new technology available for workshops, creative design, training and development.

Café and restaurant

The Doocot Café is situated on the fifth floor of The Lighthouse. Designed by Graven Images, the space has a contemporary atmosphere which is complemented by the range of organic food on the menu.

Glasgow 1999
UK City of Architecture and Design

Glasgow 1999 management team
Deyan Sudjic, Director
Eleanor McAllister, Depute Director and Project Manager
Nicole Bellamy, Exhibitions Director
Pauline Gallagher, Community Initiatives Director
Sarah Gaventa, Communications Director
Andrew Gibb, Development Director
Gordon Ritchie, Marketing Manager
Anne Wallace, Education Officer
Bruce Wood, Glasgow Collection Director

Design team
Architects Page and Park; David Paton, Colin Glover, Paul Sutton, Graeme Andrew, Frank Azemberti, Suzanne Ewing, Chris Mummery, David Page, Karen Pickering, Chris Simmonds, Fiona Service, Nicola Walls
Graphics Estudio Mariscal; Javier Mariscal
Interiors lwd; Sam Booth
Chartered Surveyors CBA; Gordon Adam, Stuart Robinson
Mechanical/Electrical Consultants Oscar Faber; Jack Devlin
Engineering Consultant Thorburn Colquhoun; Steve Harris
Main Contractor Melville Dundas; Neil Revie, Stuart McPhail, Robin Aitken
Project Management Douglas Harper
Glasgow City Council Architect Ian Duff
Lighting Jonathan Spiers Associates; Malcom Innes

The Lighthouse team
Stuart MacDonald, Director
Trevor Cromie, Exhibitions Director
Julia Fenby, Education Manager
Louise Bellin, House Manager
Susan Goldie, Marketing Manager
Bryan Sturrock, Technical Manager
Maria Pearce, Office Manager
Wendy Grubb, Community Development Officer
Dawnne McGeachy, Assistant Community Development Officer
Sarah Smith, Researcher
Angus Stewart, IT/AV Support Officer
Justin Livesey, Supervisor
Marian Roy, Adminstrative Assistant
Sarah Walker, Adminstrative Assistant
Patrick Dodds, Gallery Assistant
Pamela Flannigan, Gallery Assistant
Georgina Furst, Gallery Assistant
Craig Glass, Gallery Assistant
Lynne McGowan, Gallery Assistant
James McLardy, Gallery Assistant
Jill McNally, Gallery Assistant
Marie-Claire Miller, Gallery Assistant
Euan Mills, Gallery Assistant
Lesley Riddell, Gallery Assistant
Janice Sharp, Gallery Assistant
Daniel Willson, Gallery Assistant

Funders
Strathclyde European Partnership
Historic Scotland
Heritage Lottery Fund
Glasgow Development Agency
Glasgow City Council
Scottish Arts Council

Charles Rennie Mackintosh Centre
Gareth Hoskins, Architect
Sue Haig, Mint Design
Joe James, wigwam Digital
Mondo Ghulam, Digital Design Studio, Glasgow School of Art
Grant Hawthorn, Netherfield Visual Ltd
John Jardine, Neil Baxter Associates
Alan Crawford, Historical Consultant
Liz Arthur, Consultant
Brian Gallagher, BG Models Ltd
Cemal Ozturk, Ozturk Modelmakers

Artworks
Alexander Beleschenko, Artist (glass crafted by Franz Mayer, Munich)
Tank Design
Andy Scott, Sculptor
Digital Design Studio, Glasgow School of Art
ABACUS, Department of Architecture and Building Science, University of Strathclyde
Malcom Lindsay
Lesley Rice, Savalas
Neil Baxter Associates
Sean Gallagher, HB Signs
Peter Richardson, Zoo Architects

Sponsors
The Hugh Fraser Foundation
The Gannochy Trust
Garfield Weston Foundation
Lloyds TSB Foundation for Scotland
ICL
The Merchants House of Glasgow
The Trades House of Glasgow
Georgeson Worklife/Steelcase Strafor
Apple Macintosh
Scotsys Ltd
Allgood
Anzorg UK
Lumino
Somfy UK
Tony Walker Interiors

Other acknowledgements
Don Bennett, Glasgow City Council
Mike Hayes, formerly Glasgow City Council
Janice Kirkpatrick, Graven Images
Zoo Architects

Further information
The Lighthouse
11 Mitchell Lane
Glasgow G1 3NU
Telephone: 0141 221 6362
Fax: 0141 221 6395
Website: www.thelighthouse.co.uk
Email: enquires@thelighthouse.co.uk

This project was part-financed by the European Community